Nigerian Dwarf Goats Care

Nigerian Dwarf Goats Care

Dairy Goat Information Guide to Raising Nigerian Dwarf Dairy Goats as Pets

Goat care, breeding, diet, diseases, lifespan, personality, housing and shelter, and goat management facts.

By Taylor David

Dairy Goat Information Guide to
Raising Nigerian Dwarf Dairy Goats as Pets

Goat care, breeding, diet, diseases, lifespan, personality,
housing and shelter, and goat management facts.

Author: Taylor David
Published by: Windrunner Pets
windrunnerpets.com

ISBN: 978-1-927870-01-3

Foreword

In this book you will find all of the information you need to be prepared for becoming a Nigerian Dwarf Goat owner. You will find information about Nigerian Dwarf Goat care, caresheet, cages, enclosure, habitat, diet, facts, set up, food, names, pictures, info, life span, breeding, feeding and cost. After reading this book you will be an expert on Nigerian Dwarf Goats!

Acknowledgements

I would like to thank my darling children for inspiring me to write this book. I grew up on a dairy farm and was used to being around goats. It wasn't until I took my children to a 4-H show, however, that I learned about Nigerian Dwarf Goats. From the moment my children laid eyes on the goats, they were in love – it wasn't long before I was too.

Now we have two Nigerian Dwarf Goats of our own, Mindy and Kazoo, and they are part of the family. In learning about them, I realized that these goats are fascinating creatures that the world should know about.

I'd also like to extend my thanks to my spouse who supports me in my every endeavor.

Table of Contents

Chapter One: Introduction

When you think of the perfect pet, you probably imagine a furry, four-legged animal. Chances are, however, that the animal you imagined doesn't have hooves and horns. Nigerian Dwarf Goats are not particularly common as pets, but they are actually wonderful companion animals. These goats are friendly, good-natured and incredibly entertaining – they even make great pets for children!

They are also easy to keep as backyard pets in more urban settings due to their small size and disposition – perfect for homesteaders wanting fresh goat's milk, goat's milk cheese, or even goat's milk soap.

If you'd like to learn more about these animals and what makes them such great pets, keep reading!

Chapter Two: Understanding Nigerian Dwarf Goats

1.) What Are Nigerian Dwarf Goats?

Nigerian Dwarf Goats are a breed of domestic goat from West Africa. The domestic goat (*Capra aegagrus hircus)* is a subspecies of wild goats native to southwest Asia and Eastern Europe. All goats belong to the same subfamily as sheep, the subfamily Caprinae. Like sheep, goats were domesticated thousands of years ago, making them one of the oldest domesticated species of animals on earth.

There are over 300 species of goat and they are generally classified as either meat or dairy goats. The Nigerian Dwarf Goat is a miniature breed of dairy goat. Though officially considered a dairy goat by the American Dairy Goat Association (ADGA), these goats have recently become popular as pets or hobby goats. In addition to producing milk, these goats are also easy to care for due to their easy-going nature and small stature.

Nigerian Dwarf Goats do not have any significant physical differences from other domestic goat breeds except for their small stature. In fact, the ADGA has set forth height standards for both male and female Nigerian Dwarf Goats – only those goats that are *below* these height standards can be considered show quality. These goats are very trainable and, if bottle-fed, they can form very close bonds with their human companions.

2.) Facts About Nigerian Dwarf Goats

As it has already been mentioned, the Nigerian Dwarf Goat is a miniature breed of domestic dairy goat. Because domestic goats are a sub-species of wild goat, they do not have a separate scientific name. Thus, the scientific name of the Nigerian Dwarf Goat is *Capra aegagrus hircus*. These goats are native to Nigeria in West Africa, which is how they received their name. Though they were once valued for their meat, milk and skins, these goats are now also viewed as pets or companion animals.

There are currently two different height standards recognized for the Nigerian Dwarf Goat. The Nigerian Dwarf Goat Association (NDGA) and the American Dairy Goat Association have slightly different requirements for this breed. The ADGA requires does to be less than 22.5 inches (57 cm.) tall at the withers. Bucks should be no taller than 23.5 inches (60 cm.). The NDGA requires does should be between 17 and 19 inches (43 – 48 cm.) tall and no taller than 21 inches (53 cm.). Bucks should be no taller than 21 inches (53 cm.) and ideally measure between 19 and 21 inches (48 to 53 cm.) tall.

Nigerian Dwarf Goats exhibit similar conformation to large breeds, only on a smaller scale. These goats are balanced in proportion with a straight nose and upright ears and often have blue eyes. This breed has a soft coat of short to medium-length hair that comes in a variety of color patterns. Any combination of colors is acceptable for this breed except for the silver agouti pattern – this color combination is considered a minor fault because it is more typical of the pygmy goat.

As a breed, Nigerian Dwarf Goats are gentle and playful. They have a calm and even temperament which is what makes them great pets – especially for families with children. There is no significant difference in temperament between the sexes – even intact males are safe to handle. If you already keep livestock like sheep or other goats, your Nigerian Dwarf Goats should get along with them just fine. You do not necessarily need to house this breed in a separate enclosure.

a.) Nigerian Goat Milk

In spite of their small size, Nigerian Dwarf goats can produce a surprisingly large amount of milk. A healthy doe can produce up to two quarts (1.89 liters) per day. The milk these goats produce has a higher butterfat percentage (between 6 and 10%) than milk from many other dairy goat breeds – it is also higher in protein. In addition to being high in protein and butterfat, the milk from these goats also has a sweet flavor.

b.) Summary of Nigerian Dwarf Goats Facts

Scientific Name: *Capra aegagrus hircus*
Goat Type: Dairy
Height (Does): 17 to 22 inches (43 to 57 cm.)
Height (Bucks): 19 to 23 inches (48 to 59 cm.)
Colors: black, white, red, cream, brown
Patterns: solid, buckskin, chamoisee, spotted, frosted
Milk Production: up to 8 lbs. per day
Temperament: gentle and easily trained
Other Uses: therapy animals, companion animals

c.) Helpful Terms to Know

Dairy Goat = breeds of goat raised and bred for milk production.

Doe = a female goat

Buck = a male goat

Wether = castrated male goat

Kid = offspring of goats

Nanny = another name for female goats

Billy = another name for male goats

3.) History of Nigerian Dwarf Goats as Pets

Goats are widely known to be one of the earliest animals to be domesticated. The Bezoar Ibex, native to the mountains of Asia Minor and certain parts of the Middle East, is thought to be an ancestor of all modern domestic goats. Throughout the Paleolithic era, humans hunted wild game and gathered fruits, vegetables and roots from the earth. With the birth of agriculture, however, Neolithic humans began to farm and keep animals themselves.

Neolithic farmers are thought to have herded wild goats so they would have easy access to their meat and milk. The dung of wild goats was also a source of fuel for fires and the skins could be used for clothing. Throughout their history as a species, goats have been imported to countries all over the world which resulted in the development of over 300 different breeds.

The Nigerian Dwarf Goat breed originated in West Africa where it was used for its meat, milk and skins. These goats were brought to the United States on large ships, intended as food for the large cats kept on board. Goats that survived the trip were then kept in zoos and exhibited as exotic animals. Over time, this breed grew in popularity as a hobby goat because they were found to be very easy to care for. As word of these goats spread, they eventually came to be kept as pets as well as dairy goats.

4.) Types of Nigerian Dwarf Goats

Baby Nigerian Dwarf Goats

Baby Nigerian Dwarf Goats are called kids and they are typically born after a gestation period lasting between 145 and 153 days. When born, kids typically weigh around 2 lbs. (0.9 kg.) but they grow very quickly. Because they grow so quickly, it is possible for young bucklings to be fertile as early as 7 weeks of age. Thus, it is important to separate male and female kids very early on.

Nigerian Dwarf Goat kids are typically born in groups of 3 to 5 – 3 or 4 kids at a time is most common. The babies suckle from the dam for up to three months, at which point they should be weaned. Baby goats can accept grain and hay starting at two weeks of age but they will continue to suckle for another 6 to 8 weeks.

If you are using your Nigerian Dwarf Goats for milk production, you may need to bottle-feed the kids because there will not be enough milk available for them to nurse appropriately. When bottle feeding kids, they should be given four meals a day for the first three weeks and then three meals a day thereafter, supplemented with solid foods.

Juvenile Nigerian Dwarf Goats

Most Nigerian Dwarf Goat kids are naturally weaned by the age of 3 months. If they are not, however, this is the time you need to wean them yourself. At this point it is important to monitor the goat's intake of food to make sure it continues to gain weight properly and remains healthy. You should already have separated the bucks from the does at this point to prevent unwanted breeding. If you do not plan to breed the bucks, they should be wethered (neutered) before they reach 8 weeks of age.

Adult Nigerian Dwarf Goats

Once they reach maturity, adult Nigerian Dwarf Goats typically measure less than 21 inches (53 cm.) tall. A doe usually grows to between 17 and 19 inches (43 to 48 cm.) tall and a buck between 19 and 21 inches (48 to 53 cm.) tall. Adult goats exhibit a wide range of colors and patterns, all of which are deemed acceptable except for a white agouti coloring because it is the characteristic coloring of pygmy goats.

Male Nigerian Dwarf Goats

Bucks and wethers are particularly susceptible to urinary blockages caused by calculi – this condition can be very painful for the goats and the only effective treatment is surgery. To prevent this condition, it is wise to supplement the diet of male goats with ammonium chloride. If you cannot find a suitable supplement, adding a small amount of vinegar to the goat's water may have the same effect.

Some experienced breeders suggest that it may lower the risk for urinary blockage in male goats if they aren't wethered until at least 4 months of age – this allows the urinary tract to mature properly. To prevent accidental breeding, it is imperative that bucks be separated from does between 7 and 12 weeks of age. If possible, it is important that bucks not be housed alone. Nigerian Dwarf Goats are herding animals so a buck should be kept with another buck or a wether as a companion.

When they reach 3 months of age, bucks are capable of breeding. Many breeders choose to wait, however, until the buck is fully grown at 7 or 8 months of age. Nigerian Dwarf Goat bucks are eager breeders and they can be utilized for pasture breeding (one buck kept with several females) or more contained breeding.

Experience goat owners typically do not recommend keeping intact bucks as pets. Wethers, on the other hand, make excellent pets. The reasons intact bucks do not make good pets are numerous – though they can still be handled, bucks will eventually display a number of displeasing characteristic and behaviors. For example, as your buck grows he will begin to develop a distinct odor. The odor may not be strong at first but eventually it can become overpowering and it will stick to your skin and clothes if you pet your buck.

Another downside to keeping intact bucks is that they go into "rut" as they mature. This is the male equivalent of heat and it typically begins in the fall. During rut, a buck will spray urine on his legs and face to attract a doe. Eventually, the buck's face and legs will be covered in a sticky layer of urine-soaked fur – once the rut season is over in winter, your buck may or may not discontinue his urine-spraying behavior.

Though Nigerian Dwarf Goats are a very friendly breed, intact males may become slightly aggressive as they mature. Though you may not experience major behavioral problems, your buck may challenge you (or other goats) from time to time. Even if your buck doesn't act aggressively on purpose, they will grow stronger as they mature and accidents do happen. If you do keep a buck as a pet, it is wise to be very careful around him so you are not caught off guard.

Female Nigerian Dwarf Goats

Female Nigerian Dwarf Goats can be bred all year round – most goat breeders breed their does once or twice a year. Once a doe reaches 7 to 8 months of age, she is considered sexually mature and can be bred. Some breeders, however, prefer to wait until the doe is 1 year old before breeding her. A doe is capable of having several kids at once, even as many as 5 at a time. The most common number s are 3 or 4.

Nigerian Dwarf Goat dams make excellent mothers, caring for their babies and raising them on their own. If you do not use your goats for milk, the dam will be able to provide up to 8 cups (2 quarts) of milk per day which is sufficient to suckle several kids. In order for your goat dams to be able to provide for their kids, you need to make sure to feed the does enough – lactating and pregnant does have higher energy requirements and may need additional feeding while they are nursing their young.

5.) Nigerian Dwarf Goats vs. Pygmy Goats

If you are interested in keeping goats as pets, you are probably familiar with the pygmy goat. Pygmy goats, like Nigerian Dwarf Goats, are descendent from wild goats that were domesticated by humans. These two types of goats, though similar in origin, are separate breeds bred for separate purposes. While Nigerian Dwarf Goats can be raised for milk, pygmy goats are primarily bred for meat. Both breeds can, however, be kept as pets.

Other differences between the two breeds can be found in their appearance. Both breeds are small, though pygmy goats tend to be bred heavier. Because pygmy goats are often used for meat, they are bred to be compact and heavy-boned. Nigerian Dwarf Goats, however, are bred to have long bodies and more elegant structure like larger dairy goats. The coloring of these two breeds may also be different. While both breeds exhibit a wide range of colors, pygmy goats tend to have "agouti" coloring.

Chapter Three: What to Know Before You Buy

1.) Do You Need a License?

Before you go out and buy a Nigerian Dwarf Goat, you need to check with your local council to find out if there are any existing zoning laws or regulations prohibiting you from doing so. Depending where you live, goats may be considered livestock or small animals – you may be required to fulfill certain requirements or it might be illegal to keep them altogether. To prevent problems later, it is best to navigate the legality of keeping goats on your property before you buy them.

a.) Licensing in the U.S.

Whether or not you need to obtain a permit to keep Nigerian Dwarf Goats in the U.S. depends which state you live in. While there are no federal laws restricting the possession or breeding of these goats, some states require individual owners to file an application for a license or permit. In most cases, Nigerian Dwarf Goats are classified as "domestic animals" rather than "wildlife," so keeping of these animals is not prohibited. You should, however, check with your local council to see whether certain zoning restrictions apply.

Depending where you live, zoning regulations may require you to set aside a certain amount of space for your goats. You may also need to post a sign to let your neighbors know that you intend to purchase and keep goats. One of the most important regulations you may be required to follow is in regard to the method of enclosure. Certain cities like Chicago and Seattle have begun to allow the keeping of goats as long as they are properly contained.

If you aren't sure whether goats are allowed in your city or not, contact your local zoning department. Many cities have zoning regulations prohibiting farm animals like cows, horses and sheep but Nigerian Dwarf Goats may be considered small animals, in the same category as cats and dogs.

Ask for a copy of the zoning regulations to see whether goats are specifically mentioned and whether there are any requirements for keeping them – for example, a minimum lot size may be required to keep goats. If you are able to determine that goats are not allowed in your area, do not despair. It may be possible to get a formal exemption --- contact your local council to inquire about the process for obtaining one.

b.) Licensing in the U.K.

The legal requirements for keeping Nigerian Dwarf Goats in the U.K. are much more extensive than they are in the U.S. The reason for this is that the Animal Welfare Act of 2006 introduced legal requirements regarding the responsible care and keeping of animals. In order to uphold the Act, a number of legal requirements were put into place – these requirements apply to all goat owners in the U.K.

The Animal Welfare Act 2006 states that an animal's basic needs include:

- A suitable environment
- A suitable diet

- The ability to exhibit normal patterns of behavior
- Protection from pain, suffering, disease and injury
- Appropriate housing with or apart from other animals

In addition to providing for the basic needs of your Nigerian Dwarf Goats, you must also comply with several legal requirements. Before you purchase your goats, you must obtain a holding number (CPH) and a herd number – application for these numbers is free and can be filed with your local Department for Environment, Food and Rural Affairs (DEFRA) office. In addition to obtaining these numbers, you must also keep medical records of individual goats as well as a holding register.

When purchasing your goats, the breeder or seller is required to obtain an Animal Movement License (AML) – this license must be filled out before moving the animal. The only exception for obtaining this license is for taking the goat to the vet. Once you take up ownership of the goat, it is your responsibility to file an AML every time you move the goat off your property such as to shows or for sale.

Before a goat can be sold, it must be identified with an ear tag. The tag must include the herd number as well as a number for the individual animal. Starting in 2008, goats are required to have two forms of identification – one ear tag and a second form of identification, either another ear tag or an ear tattoo. When you tag the goat, you must record the date in your holding register.

Finally, when one of your goats dies you must record the date in your holding register. You must then have the goat removed from the premises by a licensed collector or you must take the goat yourself to a pet crematorium. As of 2011, it is now legal for goat owners to keep the ashes of their cremated pets. All of these laws are in place to ensure the safety of domestic animals and to prevent the spread of disease.

Note: Legislation may change from time to time so it is wise to check with DEFRA or with your local council regarding licensing for Nigerian Dwarf Goats.

2.) How Many Should You Buy?

Nigerian Dwarf Goats are herding animals which means they should be kept in groups with others of their own kind. Before you go out and purchase several goats, however, it is important to think about what gender ratio you will keep. Intact male goats, bucks, cannot be kept with females or with other intact males. If you plan to keep male goats, it is best to keep an intact male with a wether for companionship. Female goats can be kept in groups and wethers can be kept with female goats as well.

Intact Males = should not be kept with females or other intact males; best kept with a wether for companionship

Females = should be kept with at least 1 other female or wether for companionship

Wethers = should be kept with at least 1 other wether or female goat for companionship

3.) Can They Be Kept with Other Pets?

Like most goats, Nigerian Dwarf Goats are very friendly creatures. In addition to making great pets, these goats can also get along with other animals – particularly other livestock. This breed is typically very peaceful with other livestock including sheep, cows and other goat breeds. In fact, they are incredibly useful as pasture animals because they will feed on the brambles and weeds that other livestock tend to avoid. These goats may also get along with dogs and other pets but you should supervise their interactions to prevent accidental injury.

4.) Ease and Cost of Care

Most experienced goat owners find that Nigerian Dwarf Goats are a very easy breed to keep. Not only are these goats very friendly and gentle by nature, but their small size means that they do not require a great deal of space. Depending on the number of goats you keep, you may not need more than an enclosed pasture and a few large dog houses to provide your goats with shelter when they need it. Before you purchase a goat, however, you should take the time to learn the costs associated with keeping these animals as pets so you can determine whether it is a good choice for you.

a.) Initial Costs

The initial costs of keeping Nigerian Dwarf Goats include those costs necessary to get started. This includes the cost of building an enclosure and the requisite shelter for your goats as well as the cost of purchasing the goats themselves. You should also be prepared to cover fees for veterinary procedures such as disbudding, neutering and vaccinations, depending on the age and condition of the goats you buy. Don't forget about additional costs for equipment and accessories that you will need throughout the life of your goats.

Enclosure

Depending on the zoning requirements for your region, you will probably need to build an enclosure for your Nigerian Dwarf Goats if you do not already have a livestock enclosure in place. The cost for this varies greatly depending on the size of the pasture you intend to enclose and the materials you use. It is important that you choose quality fencing material to keep your goats in and predators out – you may also want to make sure the fence is high enough that your goats can't jump over it. You should expect to pay between $100 and $1,000 (£76 to £756) to build an enclosure for your goats.

Shelter

The type of shelter you need for your goats will depend on the climate in which you live. Nigerian Dwarf Goats do not like to get wet, so you will need some kind of shelter with a roof. These goats do not do well in four-walled enclosures, but you should provide something like a small barn or a large dog house, particularly if you live in a cold climate. The cost for shelter may range from $50 to $300 (£38 to £227) depending on size and materials.

Purchase Price

Nigerian Dwarf Goats range in price depending on age, sex and breeding. For example, a wether may be less expensive than other goats, averaging around $100 (£75). Bucks, on the other hand, may cost between $150 and $250 (£113 to £190) while a doe might cost from $250 to $300 (£189 to £227). If the goat doesn't come with a health certificate, you may need to buy one for around $50 (£38).

Veterinary Procedures

Depending on the age of the goat you purchase, or if you are breeding the goats yourself, you may need to cover the cost of some veterinary procedures. One procedure is disbudding – removing the horns from goat kids before they grow in. To have a vet perform this procedure may cost between $50 and $75 (£38 to £57) – you can also purchase a disbudding iron for around $100 (£75) to do the procedure yourself. If you are raising goat kids, you might also need to have them neutered. Again, the cost depends on the method you choose but if you have a vet perform the procedure it generally costs between $50 and $75 (£38 to £57) per goat.

Vaccinations

The cost for goat vaccinations varies depending whether you have a veterinarian administer the vaccines or if you do them yourself. If you buy the vaccine and administer it yourself, it could cost as low as $5 (£3.80)– a veterinary visit to administer the vaccine, however, could cost $30 (£23) or more.

Equipment and Accessories

Some of the equipment and accessories you should plan to buy for your goats include hoof trimmers, water and food troughs and milking equipment if you plan to use your goats for milk. Costs for equipment and accessories may range from $20 to $250 (£15 to £190).

b.) Summary of Initial Costs

Cost	Wether	Buck	Doe
Enclosure	$100-$1,000 (£76-£756)	$100-$1,000 (£76-£756)	$100-$1,000 (£76-£756)
Shelter	$50- $300 (£38-£227)	$50- $300 (£38-£227)	$50- $300 (£38-£227)
Purchase Price	$100 (£75)	$150-$250 (£113- £190)	$250-$300 (£189-£227)
Vet. Procedures	$100-$150 (£75-£114)	$50-$75 (£38-£57)	$50-75 (£38-£57)
Vaccinations	$5-$30 (£3.80-£23)	$5-$30 (£3.80-£23)	$5-$30 (£3.80-£23)
Equip./Accessories	$20-$250 (£15-£190)	$20-$250 (£15-£190)	$20-$250 (£15-£190)
Total	**$375-$1830 (£284-£1387)**	**$375-$1905 (£284-£1444)**	**$375-$1905 (£284-£1444)**

c.) Monthly Costs

After covering the initial costs for preparing for and purchasing your goats, you need to think about the monthly costs of keeping them. The monthly costs you should be prepared for include food and regular veterinary care. You might also want to figure in some additional costs that may not occur on a monthly basis such as emergency veterinary care, booster shots, and more.

Food

Because Nigerian Dwarf Goats are small, they do not need as much food as other types of livestock. The kinds of food you need to provide include hay, grain and alfalfa pellets. A single bale of hay costs between $3 and $8 (£2.27-£6) and one bale, depending on the size, should last a single goat one month. Goat feed, such as grain or alfalfa pellets, costs between $10 and $15 (£7.50-£11) per month while the cost of mineral supplements is about $5 (£3.80) per month. Add all of these costs together and you may be looking at an average cost between $18 and $28 (£13-£21) per goat per month.

Veterinary Care

As long as you care for your goats properly, you should not have to worry about veterinary care on a regular basis. If you provide a healthy diet, properly administer vaccinations and hoof trimming yourself, you may only need to consult a veterinarian in cases of emergency or illness. Assuming this to be the case, you may want to prepare for an average cost between $50 and $250 (£38 - £190) which averages to $4 – $21 (£3 - £16) per month.

Medications

Nigerian Dwarf Goats do not require many medications. One thing you may want to give them, however, is deworming medicine which typically costs about $60 (£45) per year which averages to $5 (£3.80) per month.

Additional Costs

Some additional costs you may need to pay on a monthly or yearly basis include the cost of bedding, repairs to the enclosure and replacement of tools and equipment. On a monthly basis, these costs should not be more than $15 to $30 (£11 - £23)

d.) Summary of Monthly Costs

Cost	Wether	Buck	Doe
Food	$18- $28 (£13-£21)	$18- $28 (£13-£21)	$18- $28 (£13-£21)
Veterinary Care	$4 – $21 (£3 - £16)	$4 – $21 (£3 - £16)	$4 – $21 (£3 - £16)
Medications	$5 (£3.80)	$5 (£3.80)	$5 (£3.80)
Additional Costs	$15-$30 (£11-£23)	$15-$30 (£11-£23)	$15-$30 (£11-£23)
Total	**$42 - $84 (£32 - £64)**	**$42 - $84 (£32 - £64)**	**$42 - $84 (£32 - £64)**

5.) Pros and Cons of Nigerian Dwarf Goats

As is true of all pets, Nigerian Dwarf Goats have their pros and cons. By taking the time to familiarize yourself with the pros and cons of these animals before you buy, you can make sure that these pets are the right choice for you.

Pros of Nigerian Dwarf Goats

- Small in stature; require less space than other livestock
- Very friendly and gentle personalities
- Make excellent companion pets, even for children
- Can be kept with other livestock peacefully
- Produce up to 2 quarts of milk per day
- Milk is higher in butterfat than the milk of most other dairy breeds (6-10%)
- Fairly easy to breed; produce 3 to 5 kids with each birthing
- Come in a variety of colors and patterns
- Can be trained fairly easily
- May help improve pastures by eating the weeds and brush other livestock leave behind
- Fairly inexpensive to purchase and maintain

Cons of Nigerian Dwarf Goats

- Must be kept in an enclosed area to keep predators out
- Cannot be kept in barns – need open air to be healthy
- Should not be kept alone – best kept in pairs or in groups
- Males and females cannot be kept together except for breeding purposes
- Very curious; can jump very high and may escape from the enclosure
- Intact males may develop an overpowering odor

Chapter Four: Purchasing Nigerian Dwarf Goats

1.) Where to Buy Nigerian Dwarf Goats

When you are ready to buy your goats there are a number of options to choose from. If you live in a rural area, you may not need to look any further than a local farm. Because Nigerian Dwarf Goats are still fairly rare, however, you might need to do a little bit of research. Methods of purchasing these goats vary slightly between the United States and the U.K., so follow the suggestions in the section corresponding to your location:

a.) Buying in the U.S.

In the United States you have a number of options for purchasing Nigerian Dwarf Goats. If you perform a simple online search you will find a number of farms specializing in the breeding of these animals. Before buying a goat, however, you should ensure that the breeder you are purchasing from is reputable. If you live in a rural area, ask around for referrals or get a recommendation from your veterinarian.

Another option is to check some of the national or state goat association websites. The American Nigerian Dwarf Dairy Association (ANDDA) website, for example, provides a link to a breeder directory organized by state. This list provides the names and contact information for dozens of breeders across the U.S. who are registered with the ANDDA. You may also be able to obtain breeder information from the American Dairy Goat Association (ADGA).

A less conventional option for obtaining a Nigerian Dwarf Goat may be to find a local goat rescue. Perform an online search or contact your local council regarding goat rescues in your area – you may also be able to obtain information from your local ASPCA shelter. Adopting a goat is an excellent option because the goat is likely already disbudded and neutered – it may also a be less expensive option than buying from a breeder.

If you are looking for a reputable Nigerian Dwarf Goat breeder, the first place you should look is the British Goat Society (BGS). The BGS provides its members with the opportunity to advertise on the website and may also be able to provide you with a list of breeders in your area. You may also want to ask your veterinarian if he knows of any reputable goat breeders.

Another option is to contact the Royal Society for the Prevention of Cruelty to Animals (RSPCA). The RSPCA runs animal shelters throughout the U.K. and they may have Nigerian Dwarf Goats in need of adoption. If you are looking for a pet goat and do not want to go through the hassle of weaning, disbudding and neutering a goat, you may want to consider adopting an adult goat.

One place you should be careful about obtaining goats is at livestock markets. In the case of livestock markets, and newspaper or magazine ads, you cannot be completely sure that the animal you are purchasing has been properly bred. You can examine the animal for general signs of good health but you do not know the conditions in which the animal was kept or the diseases it may have been exposed to. Your best options are to purchase from a reputable breeder or to adopt from the RSPCA.

Note: Purchasing animals online and having them shipped is typically considered animal cruelty. You have no control over the environment to which the animals are exposed or over the method of handling. Whenever possible, avoid purchasing animals online.

2.) How to Select a Healthy Nigerian Dwarf Goat

Before you purchase your goats from a breeder or seller, you should take the time to inspect the goat yourself. Look for any signs that the goat is not in peak condition – if the goat doesn't appear to be completely healthy, do not buy it. When buying goat kids, it can be tempting to buy the first kid that catches your eye and comes over the play. It is dangerous to form an attachment to a goat before you determine that it is completely healthy – it is not worth it to buy a goat that isn't healthy because you will only end up paying extra for treatment and the goat may die anyway.

When examining a goat prior to purchase, look for the following signs:

- Clear, bright eyes
- Sleek, glossy coat (no evidence of parasites)
- Clean under the tail (no evidence of diarrhea)
- No discharge coming from the nose or eyes
- Posture is strong and alert
- Feet are healthy and in good condition
- Goat is able to walk freely and easily
- Udder is spherical and free from lumps

You may also want to take the time to ask the breeder or seller some questions. If you can, take a look around the property to make sure that the goats have been kept in clean, healthy conditions. If you are purchasing a kid, ask to see the parents so you can determine whether they are in good health or not – this will be an additional indicator of the health of the kid.

Inquire as to the appetite and behavior of the goat you are thinking about purchasing. Does it have a healthy appetite? If it is a kid, has it been fully weaned? If, after asking questions, you are able to determine that the breeder is knowledgeable and that the goat itself is healthy, you can proceed to purchase it.

3.) Safely Transporting Goats

Once you have purchased your goat, the next step is to transport it home safely. Goats can be sensitive creatures, stressed or frightened by changes to their environment. For this reason, it is important to be very careful when transporting your goat. Try to make the journey as short and as safe as you can for your goat and do not make any unnecessary journeys to avoid overstressing your goat.

The first thing you need to consider in transporting goats is the safety of the transport vehicle. You should never use a vehicle that is not specifically designed for carrying livestock because it could put your goat at risk. If you have your own goat trailer, or if you are borrowing one, you should always clean the trailer and disinfect it before using it. This will reduce the risk of disease transmission from one goat to another and from one herd to another.

The floor of the trailer should be covered in some kind of non-slip material to prevent your goats from falling. Additionally, you should provide some soft bedding such as straw or hay for your goats. You should also take the time to inspect the inside of the trailer for any protruding handles or bolts that your goats could run into. Take the time to remove or shield these items so your goats can move safely around the trailer.

Because Nigerian Dwarf Goats are so small, loading them into the trailer is fairly easy. These goats can generally be lifted into the trailer or they can be led up a ramp. The ramp itself, if you are using one, should also be lined with non-slip material. Use caution when unloading your goats because they may be stressed or agitated by the journey. Be sure to prepare a fenced route to lead your goats from their enclosure to and from the trailer so they do not escape.

The day before you make the journey, take the time to choose a safe route. If you can, avoid heavily-travelled areas because your goats may be stressed by the noise and jostle of traffic. When driving, make every effort to accelerate and break smoothly so as to reduce the chances of your goats falling over in the trailer. For short journeys, you do not need to provide food or water for your goats in the trailer but you should give them access to these provisions as soon as you arrive at your destination.

Note: Remember, in the U.K. you will need to obtain an Animal Moving License (AML) before transporting your goats.

Chapter Five: Caring for Nigerian Dwarf Goats

1.) Habitat Requirements

Nigerian Dwarf Goats are not complicated creatures so they do not require an extravagant habitat. All that they need is space to roam, food to forage and shelter from the weather. There are three main areas that can be used for keeping Nigerian Dwarf Goats. The first option is to keep your goats in a large, fenced-off pasture. The pasture will give your goats space to run and play as well as food to forage. If you choose this option you should be sure that there are no poisonous plants in the area and that it is secure from predators.

Another option is to take a small field and divide it into several portions using fencing. You can keep the goats in one area and, as they consume the foliage in that portion, move them to the next. This method is called rotational pasturing and it ensures that the foliage in one area is able to regrow before the goats return.

For a small number of goats, a large yard may also be acceptable. The benefits of this option are that it is easily contained, parasites may not proliferate the soil as easily as in a pasture and the ground may be rough enough to help ground down the goats' hooves naturally. On the other hand, there is little food for your goats to forage so you will have to bring all of their food to them – you will also have to supply fresh water and an area where the goats can play and exercise.

a.) Shelter for Goats

Nigerian Dwarf Goats do not like getting wet so it is important that you provide them with a shelter from rain. Your goats should have access to shelter at all times – either by leaving the main goat house accessible or by constructing temporary shelters in the enclosure. The main goat house should be a four-walled enclosure where you can keep your goats secured at night and during bad weather. It is not a good idea to keep your goats in the goat house for extended periods of time, but it is a good idea to have one when you need it.

In both the main goat house and temporary shelters you should provide plenty of soft bedding. The shelter itself should be large enough to accommodate all of your goats at one time. The ideal construction materials for a goat shelter include wood, stone, concrete or a mixture of these materials – metal is not a good material to use because it will get very hot in the summer and very cold during the winter. In regards to space, a goat shelter should provide at least 2 square meters (6 square feet) of floor space per goat.

The roof of the goat shelter needs to be leak-proof to keep out rain. You should also be sure to provide proper ventilation in the shelter without creating draughts. To make cleaning the shelter easier, the floor should be made of concrete and slightly sloped – after removing the bedding it can be easily washed clean. The ideal bedding for Nigerian Dwarf Goats is straw, though peat or wood shavings can also be used. The bedding should be mucked out and replaced about once a week, depending on the number of goats you keep.

b.) Adequate Fencing

While having a shelter for your goats is important, they will spend most of their time outside. It is important that you provide enough space for your goats to roam and exercise, but the area should be fenced off to keep the goats from escaping and to keep predators from getting in. Ideally, you should provide at least 8.5 square meters of outdoor space per goat – this will give them enough room to run without feeling confined.

In terms of the fence itself, it should be very strong and durable. Goats are excellent jumpers and climbers – though Nigerian Dwarf Goats may be small, they may surprise you in their abilities as escape artists. For this reason hedges and stone walls are not good options for fencing. To build an enclosure for goats, use strong wood or metal vertical posts that are driven well into the ground. For the fencing itself, use chain link or galvanized wire mesh with small enough apertures that your goats cannot fit their heads, legs or bodies through the gaps.

Warning: Electrical livestock fencing can be used for goats to provide additional protection from predators but you need to be very careful when installing it – you should also take care that your goats do not come into contact with the fence often. Barbed wire fences are never a good option for goats because they may try to jump over them, becoming tangled.

c.) Playgrounds for Goats

Nigerian Dwarf Goats have a natural curiosity and a playful demeanor. They love to climb and explore so they would enjoy the addition of a "playground" to their enclosure. A playground for dwarf goats need not be extravagant – it can be made up of tree stumps, old tires, wooden benches and even scrap wood. Use your creativity to provide some enrichment for your goats by creating a playground for them to enjoy.

d.) Summary of Habitat Requirements

Habitat Options: fenced-off pasture, rotational pasture, large yard

Minimum Outdoor Space: 8.5 square meters per goat

Minimum Indoor Space: 2 square meters per goat

Fencing Materials: wood or metal posts; chain link or galvanized wire mesh fencing

Shelter Materials: wood, stone, concrete

Shelter Specifications: well-ventilated, leak-proof roof, sloped concrete floor, soft bedding

Extras: playground for exercise

2.) Breeding Nigerian Dwarf Goats

It is not difficult to breed Nigerian Dwarf Goats but that does not necessarily mean that everyone should do it. Breeding goats is a big responsibility and if you do not do it correctly, it could result in serious consequences. Pregnant does have specific dietary needs and the birthing process may require the assistance of a veterinarian or experienced goat owner. Caring for the kids can also be a challenge because you need to be able to house the males and females separately, not to mention arranging for the necessary procedures such as castrating and disbudding.

If you have experience breeding other kinds of goats, or if you have done your research and feel that you are up to the challenge, breeding Nigerian Dwarf Goats can be a very rewarding experience. It is incredibly entertaining to watch young kids interact and it is also a great opportunity to form a bond with your goats while they are very young. If you do plan to breed your goats, do yourself a favor and take the time to learn how to do it correctly.

a.) Basic Breeding Info

Nigerian Dwarf Goats can be bred all year round. A doe typically reaches sexual maturity between 7 and 8 months of age, though some breeders choose to wait a full year before breeding. Female goats should not be bred until they reach at least 60% to 75% of their adult weight. This will reduce the risk for difficult kidding. Male goats, on the other hand, can become fertile as early as 7 weeks of age but generally are not bred until they are at least 3 months old. Though Nigerian Dwarf Goats can breed continuously, it is best to give the doe a 6-month break between kiddings.

Female goats go into heat (estrus) every 18 to 21 days and the cycle itself lasts 2 to 3 days. This is the ideal time for breeding because it ensures the greatest likelihood of conception. Once conception has occurred, the gestation period begins and lasts 143 to 151 days. At birth, Nigerian Dwarf Goat kids typically weigh about 2 lbs. (0.90 kg.) but they grow very quickly. Female goats are very good at raising their kids and most are naturally weaned before they reach 3 months of age.

b.) The Breeding Process

To ensure the greatest chance of a successful mating, it is best to attempt breeding when the doe is in heat. One of the signs of heat is a mucus discharge coming from the vulva of the female, resulting in matted hair around the tail. Other signs include frequent urination, loss of appetite and bleating. When the doe is ready for breeding, it is best to introduce the doe to the buck – take the female to the male instead of the other way around. Many goat breeders recommend two to four breeding sessions per estrus cycle to ensure conception.

Mature bucks can be mated many times a year. For bucks only one or two years old, it is recommended that you limit them to 25 services per year. Older bucks, however, can do up to 75 doe services a year. When you are ready to breed your Nigerian Dwarf Goats, record the date of the mating so you can predict the birth of the kids. This is important because, if the kidding becomes difficult for the doe, you should be around to help.

c.) Raising the Babies

It can be difficult to predict exactly when your does will give birth. There are, however, a few signs you can look for. A mucus discharge from the vulva is the most obvious sign of pre-kidding. After the kids are born, it is important that they suckle from their mother as soon as possible. The first milk produced after birth is called colostrum and it contains high quantities of antibodies, vitamins and minerals that are essential for newborn kids.

In most cases, the doe will raise the kids herself and you should not have to do much. It is okay to let the kids nurse for as long as they like because they will likely wean themselves before they reach 3 months of age. Nigerian Dwarf Goat kids may begin grazing as early as 2 weeks of age and will eventually start consuming more solid food and less milk from their dam. Weaning can be stressful on kids, so it is important to keep a close eye on them during this period.

d.) Breeding Info Summary

Does

Sexual Maturity: 7 to 8 months
Breeding Weight: 60% to 75% of adult weight
Estrus: 18 to 22 days
Length of Cycle: 2 to 3 days
Signs of Heat: bleating, frequent urination, lack of appetite
Gestation Period: 143 to 151 days
Number of Kids: average 3 to 4 (up to 5)
Size of Newborns: 2 lbs. (0.90 kg.)

Bucks

Sexual Maturity: 4 to 8 months (may become fertile as early as 7 weeks of age)
Ideal Breeding Age: 8 to 10 months
Breeding Season: all year
Breeding Ratio: 1 buck per 25 does

3.) Feeding Nigerian Dwarf Goats

In many cases, Nigerian Dwarf Goats are more than just pets – they can also be used for milk or to help keep pastures from becoming overgrown. If you do plan to keep your goats in a pasture, you may still need to supplement their diet. Even though goats will eat weeds and brush, these foods may not satisfy all of their nutritional needs.

The general needs of Nigerian Dwarf Goats include:

- Access to clean water

- A constant supply of quality hay
- Daily supplementation of non-toxic greens
- Daily ration of concentrates (pellets)
- Daily mineral supplements
- A regular feeding routine

a.) Nutritional Needs

One of the most important needs Nigerian Dwarf Goats have is for fresh, clean water. These goats tend not to accept water that has been dirtied so you may need to check their water several times a day and refresh it if necessary. You should be careful about where you place water troughs and buckets so the goats do not accidentally urinate or defecate in them – if they do, the water should be changed immediately. Generally, goats prefer water that is slightly warm. A single goat can consume 4 to 6 gallons (18 to 27 liters) of water a day.

In addition to fresh water, your goats need a supply of fresh hay. Nigerian Dwarf Goats are ruminant animals which means their stomachs have several compartments, one of which is designed to soften fibrous plant foods. The first compartment of the stomach is called the rumen and it contains bacteria that helps to break down plant material. The plant material is then regurgitated and then chewed again to break it down further for digestion.

Fibrous foods such as hay should make up about 50% of a goat's diet. This hay should be fresh and free from signs of mold – a 40-pound (18 kg) bale of hay will last a single Nigerian Dwarf Goat about one month. Aside from hay, another 25% of your goat's diet should be made up of extra vegetation such as grass, roots, branches and other non-toxic plant foods. In order for a goat's rumen to work properly, they need to eat long, fibrous foods – thus, when giving your goat grass or hay it should be at least 4 inches (10 cm.) long.

If you do not plan to breed your Nigerian Dwarf Goats, a diet composed of hay and other plant materials should be sufficient. If additional plant material is in short supply, or if you are raising kids or using your goats for milking, you may want to supplement their diets with concentrates. Concentrates are a type of commercial food, often in the form of pellets, which provide goats with additional vitamins and minerals. When feeding your goats concentrates it is essential that you also provide plenty of long hay or grass so they can properly digest the concentrates.

Note: An adult goat does not need a lot of concentrate in its diet – feeding too much can lead to obesity and, in males, the development of urinary tract issues such as bladder stones.

b.) Feeding Tips

Like many goats, Nigerian Dwarf Goats prefer not to eat food that has touched the floor. For this reason, you will need to purchase a number of hayracks. Hayracks can be found at most feed stores and farm supply stores – they can be covered with a lid to keep the hay in and should be positioned at such a height that your goats will not accidentally soil the hay inside. If you have multiple goats, you will need to buy a hayrack large enough that all of the goats can feed at once without competing for space.

Because Nigerian Dwarf Goats have very sensitive stomachs, it is important that you make any changes to their diet gradually. These goats do appreciate variety in their diet but sudden changes in dietary routine could cause digestive issues. Goats rely on the bacteria in their rumen to help digest their food – if you introduce new foods suddenly, the bacteria will not be able to digest it right away. Rather, introduce small amounts of new food so the bacteria in your goats' stomachs can adjust.

**Caution: Never use hay nets for goats – these are intended for horses and Nigerian Dwarf Goats can easily become entangled in the nets.

c.) Foods to Avoid

Nigerian Dwarf Goats tend to graze, so you need to be very careful about what plants to keep on your property. Many wild plants including weeds and grasses are edible for goats but some are extremely toxic and could kill your goats if they ingest it.

Some of the most important plants to avoid include:

Alder	Honeysuckle	Daffodils
Laurel	Walnut	Foxglove
Privet	Evergreen	Mayweed
Rhododendron	shrubs	Celandine
Yew	Tulips	Buttercup

| Hemlock | Nightshades | Laburnum |
| Ragwort | Bryony | Delphinium |

**Note: If you do have any of these plants on your property, make sure to prevent your goats from having access to them – this includes properly disposing of clippings so your goats can't get into them.

Chapter Six: Keeping Your Nigerian Dwarf Goats Healthy

1.) Common Health Problems

No matter how careful you are you can't completely protect your Nigerian Dwarf Goats from disease – they are likely to be exposed at some time. What matters most in this situation is not what you failed to do to prevent the disease, but how quickly you act to treat it.

You should spend time with your goats on a daily basis to familiarize yourself with their behavior. In doing so, you will be more likely to recognize changes in behavior or other symptoms of disease as soon as they manifest. Quick diagnosis and treatment is the key to successful recovery.

The following conditions are fairly common in domestic goats including Nigerian Dwarf Goats:

Coccidiosis

This condition is caused by protozoan parasites called *Coccidia*. This parasites can cause damage to the lining of the small intestine which often results in the malabsorption of nutrients and thus weight loss, stunted growth and/or diarrhea. Other symptoms of Coccidiosisinclude fever, anemia, dehydration, and secondary infections.

This condition tends to infect goats that are kept in close quarters or in unsanitary conditions – kids between the age of one and six months are at the greatest risk. Spread of the disease can be controlled through increased sanitation efforts and through treatment with sulfa drugs.

Cause: protozoan parasites, *Coccidia*
Symptoms: dehydration, anemia, weight loss, diarrhea, stunted growth
Treatment: increased sanitation efforts and sulfa drugs

Enterotoxemia

Also known as overeating disease, enterotoxemia may manifest in several forms. This condition is almost always associated with a change in diet or a change in the quality of the feed used. Symptoms of the disease may include fever, watery diarrhea, decreased milk yield and death. If not treated within 48 hours, the condition is often fatal. Treatment for enterotoxemia may include antitoxins and antibiotics.

Cause: change in diet or change in feed quality
Symptoms: fever, watery diarrhea, decreased milk yield
Treatment: antitoxins and antibiotics

Respiratory Problems

Respiratory problems like pneumonia are most common in kids, but they can affect Nigerian Dwarf goats of any age. There are many different kinds of respiratory problems but they are most often caused by some combination of bacterial and viral agents infecting the lungs. These problems are more likely to occur in goats that are already stressed due to weaning, poor air quality, transport or a change in weather.

The most common signs of pneumonia include fever, moist cough and difficulty breathing – depression and loss of appetite may also occur. Treatment for pneumonia typically involves the administration of antibiotics but it may depend on the diagnosis. The disease can be prevented by keeping goats in dry, well-ventilated areas and by minimizing the stress to which they are exposed.

Cause: combination of viral and bacterial agents infecting the lungs; often brought on by stress
Symptoms: fever, wet cough, difficulty breathing, loss of appetite, depression
Treatment: depends on diagnosis; often antibiotics

Keratoconjunctivitis

Pinkeye, or infectious keratoconjunctivitis, is most likely to occur during warm weather. This disease is highly contagious and can easily be spread through close contact or by flies. Stress is a significant factor in the spread of this disease as are good sanitation and fly control. Common signs of the disease include redness of the eye, swelling or excess tearing – if the disease progresses, it may also result in opacity of the eye, corneal ulcers and blindness. Treatment for this disease typically involves broad-spectrum antibiotics.

Cause: spread through close contact or flies
Symptoms: redness of the eye, swelling, excess tearing

Chapter Six: Keeping Your Goats Healthy

Treatment: broad-spectrum antibiotics

Soremouth

Also called contagious ecthyma, soremouth is a type of viral skin disease. This disease is caused by a virus which enters the body through broken skin and results in infection of the mouth, nose, udder or teats. Symptoms of the disease include scabs or blisters, loss of condition, stunted growth and loss of appetite. When this condition affects the teats of lactating does it can be very harmful because it becomes painful for the doe to nurse her kids – this may result in premature weaning. In some cases, the disease will go away on its own but it can also be treated with an iodine/glycerin solution.

Cause: a virus which enters the body through broken skin
Symptoms: scabs or blisters, loss of condition, stunted growth and loss of appetite
Treatment: treatment with iodine/glycerin solution

Scours

Scours is a term used to refer to diarrheal diseases, particularly those most common in kids. These diseases are often caused by coccidia, worms, salmonella and various viruses. The symptoms of the disease vary but often include anorexia, fever, weakness and watery stools. Treatment for this condition includes antibiotics, intestinal astringents and fluid therapy. Preventive measures for scours involve good sanitation and proper housing.

Cause: coccidia, worms, salmonella and various viruses
Symptoms: anorexia, fever, weakness and watery stools
Treatment: antibiotics, intestinal astringents and fluid therapy

Mastitis

Mastitis is a bacterial infection of the mammary gland resulting in inflammation. One of the leading causes for the culling of goats and other livestock is udder damage resulting from mastitis. Symptoms of this condition include warm or swollen mammary glands, milk of abnormal color or consistency and depression. If the bacteria enter the bloodstream, the infected goat may become septic and exhibit additional symptoms such as anorexia, fever, depression and lethargy.

Though technically caused by bacteria, the risk for this disease increases with poor sanitation. A systemic infection or trauma inflicted upon the udder may also contribute to development of the disease. Treatment for mastitis often involves intramammary and system antibiotic treatment. In some cases, udder damage may occur despite treatment.

Cause: bacterial infection of the mammary gland resulting in inflammation
Symptoms: warm or swollen mammary glands, milk of abnormal color or consistency and depression
Treatment: intramammary and system antibiotic treatment

Lameness

Lameness occurs when a goat is no longer able to use one or more of its limbs. This condition is often caused by compaction of debris between the toes, injury to the legs or feet, bacterial infection of the feet, footrot or penetration of the feet by thorns or stones.

If a Nigerian Dwarf Goat begins to limp or becomes reluctant to stand up or move around it should immediately be separated from the other goats. The affected goat should be isolated, kept on dry straw and undergo inspection of the legs and feet. Treatment depends on the cause of the condition and generally must be determined by a veterinarian.

Cause: compaction of debris between the toes, injury to the legs or feet, bacterial infection of the feet, footrot or penetration of the feet by thorns or stones

Symptoms: limping, favoring one leg, reluctance to stand up or move around

Treatment: depends on the cause of the condition

Internal Parasites

Nigerian Dwarf Goats can be affected by a number of internal parasites including roundworms, tapeworms, lungworms, coccidia and nematodes. Common symptoms of internal parasite infections include diarrhea, weight loss, loss of appetite and reduced growth rates. Roundworms are the most common type of parasite affecting goats – these infections often cause anemia, edema, weakness and lethargy.

Tapeworms tend to infect the digestive tract and may result in yellowish-white stools. Tapeworm infections are most common in kids under four months of age because kids quickly develop a resistance to them. Treatment for internal parasite infections vary from one disease to another but deworming medications are the most common.

Cause: roundworms, tapeworms, lungworms, coccidia and nematodes

Symptoms: diarrhea, weight loss, loss of appetite and reduced growth rates

Treatment: deworming medications

External Parasites

External parasite infections often manifest in the form of skin problems. Some of the most common external parasites are lice and mites. These infections are most common in winter when Nigerian Dwarf Goats are kept indoors in close quarters. Various parasites affect goats in different ways. Chewing lice, for example, feed on dead skin cells while sucking lice feed on the animal's blood. Mites burrow into the skin, causing itching, skin irritation, hair loss and scabs or lesions. Treatment may include topical insecticides or injectable Ivermectin.

Cause: lice and mites

Symptoms: itching, skin irritation, hair loss and scabs or lesions

Treatment: topical insecticides or injectable Ivermectin.

Footrot

Also called foot scald, footrot is a bacterial infection affecting the foot of goats. This infection is caused by either *Fusobacterium necrophorum* or *Dichelobacter nodus* and it is most common in warm, most areas. In virulent cases, the bacteria actually enter the hoof, digesting the horny sole and eating into the fleshy tissue. Common symptoms of this disease include redness of the toes, inflammation and bad odor. In extreme cases, the horn of the hoof may actually separate from the hoof wall. If left untreated, footrot can lead to lameness, weight loss and decreased reproductive capabilities.

This condition is often introduced when a new goat is brought into the herd. Goats are more at risk for this condition when their hooves are not trimmed regularly and when they are kept in crowded conditions. Treatment options include foot soaking baths of zinc sulfate, vaccination and antibiotic treatments.

Cause: *Fusobacterium necrophorum* or *Dichelobacter nodus* bacteria
Symptoms: redness of the toes, inflammation and bad odor
Treatment: foot soaking baths of zinc sulfate, vaccination and antibiotic treatments.

2.) Preventing Illness

The best way to prevent illness in your Nigerian Dwarf Goats is to provide them with a clean habitat and a healthy diet. Another way to prevent disease is to avoid exposing your goats to other herds – most contagious diseases are introduced when new goats are added to the herd. Your goats may also be exposed to disease at a fair, during a show or even through exposure to wildlife. If you do add a goat to your herd, be sure to quarantine it for at least 30 days to make sure the animal isn't a carrier for disease.

You may also want to keep a qualified veterinarian nearby

to help you deal with Nigerian Dwarf Goat diseases. Having a trained professional available to diagnose and treat diseases is a very valuable asset. You do not necessarily need to take each of your goats in for regular visits, although having the occasional check-up can be very beneficial. During these check-ups your veterinarian will be able to recommend vaccines and may also help you to catch the symptoms of disease or nutritional deficiency before they become a problem. Your vet will also help you decide on a parasite control program.

Vaccines are another way to prevent illness in goats but they should be used with caution. The only vaccine that is universally recommended for goats is for clostridial diseases. This vaccine is not required, but many goat owners choose to administer it to their herds. Once the vaccine has been administered, boosters are recommended every 4 to 6 months. Some goat owners also choose to vaccinate against soremouth, but it is generally not necessary unless the herd has been exposed.

3.) Common Procedures

If you plan to keep Nigerian Dwarf Goats, you may need to perform these procedures from time to time:

a.) Disbudding

Disbudding is the process through which a goat's horns are removed. In most cases, this procedure is done before the goat reaches two weeks of age (typically after 10 days). Though it may sound cruel, disbudding prevents goats from injuring each other in close quarters and it makes it easier to keep them with other hornless livestock. The reason disbudding is done so early is because it is important that the root of the horn is burned out to prevent further growth. If you wait too long to disbud the goat, it will be more difficult (and more dangerous for the goat) to do so later.

Many goat owners learn how to disbud their goats themselves using a disbudding iron. Another option, however, is to have the procedure performed by a licensed veterinarian. Intravenous anesthesia should never be used on goats but an anesthetic gas called isoflurine can be used to sedate goats for the disbudding procedure. It is possible to disbud a goat after the horns have grown in but it will require surgery and a long recovery period.

b.) Hoof Trimming

If a goat's hooves aren't trimmed regularly, they can develop foot rot and may even cause the goat to become lame. Ideally, a Nigerian Dwarf Goat's hooves should be trimmed every one to two months. It is possible to trim your goat's hooves on your own, but it is best to have a professional show you how to do it the first time. You will need a pair of hoof trimmers, a hoof pick, a carpenter's plane and a pair of safety goggles to wear to prevent pieces of hoof from flying into your eyes.

Take a look at your goat's hooves – if they are overgrown, they may turn under on the sides and might even curl upward at the tip. Your first step in trimming your goat's hooves is to clean them out using a hoof pick. Once you've cleared away any mud or grass, use the hoof trimmers to clip away the overgrown edges of the hoof to expose the white sole. Next, you may want to use a toothbrush to scrub the sides of each hoof clean so you can see the growth lines for a better trim.

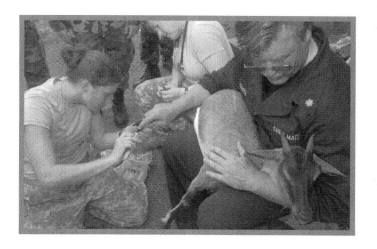

If you look closely, you will see that the growth lines are parallel with the hair at the top of the hoof – they are not parallel to the ground. Many novice goat owners make the mistake of trimming their goat's hooves at an angle parallel with the ground rather than following the growth lines. This may result in the foot rolling backwards, forcing the goat's pasterns to break down more quickly. The goat's toes grow more quickly than the heel so you should trim the hoof at an angle that takes more off the toe than the heel.

Once you've scrubbed the hooves and identified the growth lines you can begin to trim the hooves using your trimmers. Position your goat so that you can hold both of its back hooves together, side by side. Carefully use the trimmers to shear slices off the side and bottom surface of the hoof. Keep trimming until the hard white nail turns pink. You may trim the heel a little bit as well, but only enough that it is level with the same growth ring as the toe. After trimming the hooves, snip off any flaps of nail that are sticking out between the hooves.

Finally, use the carpenter's plane to level out the hooves. As you do so, you should not be alarmed if little spots of blood form on the bottom of the hoof. These tiny spots will not harm your goat but it is best to stop trimming at that point. You may also want to treat the area with iodine to prevent foot rot. With time and practice, trimming your Nigerian Dwarf Goat's hooves should become easy for you.

c.) Tethering

Tethering a goat is simply the act of tying it to a post or some other stationary object to keep the goat from wandering too far. Most goat owners advise against tethering goats for a number of reasons. First, there is always a chance that your goat could be attacked by a predator. If the goat is tethered, it will not be able to get away. Second, the goat could be strangled by the tether.

Note: If you must tether your goat, you should be sure to supervise it the entire time it is tethered. A better option is to create a small enclosure that you can use when you need to temporarily contain your goat.

d.) Wethering (Castrating)

Wethering or castrating a male goat involves removing the testicles, thus rendering the goat sterile. If a male Nigerian Dwarf Goat is left intact, he may eventually develop behavior problems and could become difficult to handle. Unless you plan to keep your bucks for breeding purposes, it is best to wether them while they are still young.

Improper wethering, or performing the procedure too early, can increase the goat's risk for developing bladder stones. For this reason, it is a good idea to wait until the goat's urethra grows properly before performing the procedure. Many goat owners wether their bucks within the first 10 days while others wait as long as four weeks, allowing the urethra to develop.

There are three different methods of neutering a male goat: cutting, banding and using a burdizzo. The cutting method involves cutting off the bottom of the scrotum and pulling out the testicles. The benefit of this method is that it is guaranteed to be effective and it is also inexpensive. On the downside, it leaves the goat susceptible to tetanus and infection.

The second method, banding, involves putting heavy rubber bands around the scrotum. The bands are put into place using a tool called an elastrator. After 10 to 14 days, blood flow to the scrotum will cease ad the scrotum and testes will slough off. The main benefit of this method is that it is very inexpensive but the downsides are that it is generally considered to be inhumane – it may also be a faulty method, resulting in the retention of one testicle.

The final method of castrating a male goat involves the use of a tool called a Burdizzo, or emasculatome. This is a clamp-like tool which is used to crush the blood vessels and spermatic cord connected to the testicles. When used correctly, this method results in loss of blood to the testicles so they eventually die. The benefit of this method is that it is "bloodless" and quick. As long as both cords have been crushed, this method is very effective and the kid will recover within 24 hours. To be sure that the procedure was effective, you should check after 4 weeks to make sure the testicles are no longer growing – they should be small and hard, not the same size or larger.

e.) Culling

Culling is a practice that is typically used by large-scale goat farmers but it may also be something you need to do on occasion if you keep a large herd of goats – particularly for breeding purposes. When a goat becomes seriously injured, infected with an untreatable disease or fails to thrive despite proper feeding, a low parasite load and healthy teeth, culling may be recommended.

Though it sounds cruel, culling infected or underperforming goats from the herd is essential if you want to protect the overall productivity of your goats as a group. If you keep individuals that are carriers for or suffering from disease, the disease could spread to others in the herd through contact or through mating – this could decrease the overall value of your herd.

4.) Behavioral Problems

Nigerian Dwarf Goats are generally friendly creatures and a pleasure to keep around. There are times, however, when certain behaviors may become an issue. It is important that you spend time with your goats on a regular basis so you become familiar with their normal behaviors – sudden changes in behavior may be an indication of illness or injury.

Common behavioral problems include:

- Vocalization
- Destructive behavior

- Head butting

Vocalization

Nigerian Dwarf Goats generally do not make a lot of noise. There are situations, however, in which they are likely to bleat or cry. When female goats go into heat, they may bleat frequently – the same is true of intact males that are not allowed access to does in heat. A goat might also bleat when it is hungry, thirsty, sick or injured. If your goat does not normally make much noise, you should take the time to investigate any changes in this behavior.

Destructive Behavior

This breed of goat is naturally curious – they also have a love for climbing and jumping. In the course of exercising and playing, it is not uncommon for Nigerian Dwarf Goats to cause some damage to their habitat. These goats may also chew on woodwork, rub against fencing and dig up the ground. To prevent your goats from hurting themselves with this behavior it is important that you use only non-toxic materials in your goat enclosure and that you reinforce the fencing to prevent escape.

Head Butting

Wild goats display their status by butting heads with their rivals. Though Nigerian Dwarf Goats are not aggressive by nature, they may occasionally exhibit head-butting behavior. This behavior may be triggered by adding a new goat to the herd or when two intact males are introduced to each other. To prevent this behavior from becoming dangerous, it is wise to have your goats disbudded at an early age.

Chapter Seven: Showing Nigerian Dwarf Goats

1.) Breed Standard

The standard for the Nigerian Dwarf Goat was published in 1996 by the American Goat Society. The breed standard states that the Nigerian Dwarf is a miniature dairy breed with conformation similar to larger dairy breeds. The body of these goats are balanced in proportion – it is considered a fault if the goat has a disproportionately large head or a large body on short legs.

The profile of the Nigerian Dwarf Goat's face should be straight, with or without a small break at eye-level. The ears should be upright and the coat straight with short to medium-length hair. All color combinations are acceptable. There are no height minimums for either sex, but does measuring over 22.4 inches (56.9 cm.) and bucks measuring over 23.6 inches (59.9 cm.) at the withers will be disqualified. Additional faults include a curly coat, Roman nose, pendulous ears and evidence of myatonia.

Note: The original standard for the breed was created in 1983 when the American Goat Society endeavored to distinguish Nigerian Dwarf Goats from Pygmy Goats. The data used to create the standard, however, were drawn from the smallest stock specimens imported from Africa – these data did not account for the fact that many goats carry genes for a broad height range. Thus, the standard was changed over time and republished in 1996.

2.) What to Know Before Showing

Nigerian Dwarf Goats are judged using the dairy scorecard and they are classified according to how well an individual specimen approaches the ideal dairy goat type. Before competing in sanctioned shows, all goats must be measured – any Nigerian Dwarf Goat not meeting the height limits will be immediately disqualified. These measurements are taken using an AGS official measuring device. The goat's height is measured from the highest point on the withers to the ground.

Judging for Nigerian Dwarf Goats is based on the dairy scorecard and values are assigned in the following categories:

General Appearance (35% senior does, 55% junior does, 55% bucks)
Mammary System (35% senior does)
Dairy Character (20% senior does, 30% junior does, 30% bucks)
Body Capacity (10% senior does, 15% junior does, 15% bucks)

Chapter Eight: Nigerian Dwarf Goats Caresheet

For a quick reference about Nigerian Dwarf Goats, check this summary of information as discussed earlier:

a.) Basic Information

Scientific Name: *Capra aegagrus hircus*

Goat Type: Dairy

Life expectancy: 8-12 years. 15 years in some cases

Height (Does): 17 to 22 inches (43 to 57 cm.)

Height (Bucks): 19 to 23 inches (48 to 59 cm.)

Colors: black, white, red, cream, brown

Patterns: solid, buckskin, chamoisee, spotted, frosted

Milk Production: up to 8 lbs. per day

Temperament: gentle and easily trained

Other Uses: therapy animals, companion animals

b.) Habitat Set-up Guide

Habitat Options: fenced-off pasture, rotational pasture, large yard
Minimum Outdoor Space: 8.5 square meters per goat
Minimum Indoor Space: 2 square meters per goat
Fencing Materials: wood or metal posts; chain link or galvanized wire mesh fencing
Shelter Materials: wood, stone, concrete
Shelter Specifications: well-ventilated, leak-proof roof, sloped concrete floor, soft bedding
Extras: playground for exercise

c.) Breeding Info and Tips

Sexual Maturity: 7 to 8 months (does), 4 to 8 months (bucks)
Breeding Weight: 60% to 75% of adult weight (does)
Estrus: 18 to 22 days
Length of Cycle: 2 to 3 days
Signs of Heat: bleating, frequent urination, lack of appetite
Gestation Period: 143 to 151 days
Number of Kids: average 3 to 4 (up to 5)
Size of Newborns: 2 lbs. (0.90 kg.)
Breeding Ratio: 1 buck per 25 does
Mating Procedure: introduce female to male

Number of Matings: 2 to 4 per cycle to ensure conception

Chapter Nine: Common Mistakes Owners Make

1.) Keeping Nigerian Dwarf Goats Alone

All goats, not just Nigerian Dwarf Goats, are herd animals. This means that they must be kept in groups in order to thrive. Two goats can be kept together happily and this breed can be kept with other livestock. Wethers and does can be kept in any combination, but intact males are best kept with a wether for companionship. Nigerian Dwarf Goats can also be used as companion pets for cows, horses and sheep.

2.) Feeding the Wrong Diet

The diet you offer your Nigerian Dwarf Goats is incredibly important. If you do not offer the right food or the right proportions of food types, your goats may fail to thrive. Goats have very sensitive stomachs and while it is often said they will eat anything, they cannot thrive on a diet of goat concentrates alone.

In order to keep your goats healthy you need to provide them with a diet containing 50% fresh hay. The remaining 50% of your goats' diet should be made up of additional vegetable matter, commercial pellets and mineral supplements. Do not make any sudden changes to your goat's diet because it could cause digestive issues.

3.) Not Disbudding or Castrating

As was discussed earlier in the book, though certain procedures like disbudding and castrating may seem cruel, the consequences of not performing these procedures can be severe. If you fail to disbud your goats, they may end up hurting themselves during exercise or play – they may also be more likely to become entangled in ropes and nets if their horns grow in. A failed disbudding is equally dangerous – if you do not perform the procedure correctly, the horns may grow in wrong and may need to be surgically removed.

Unless you plan to breed your male goats, there is little reason not to castrate them. Castrating a male goat will prevent him from developing buck-like behavior such as aggression, head butting and urine spraying. If you do castrate your male goats, you will be able to keep them together with your does rather than housing them separately to prevent unwanted breeding.

Chapter Ten: Frequently Asked Questions

General Care Questions

Q: What makes Nigerian Dwarf Goats great pets?

A: This breed makes a great companion pet for a number of reasons. Not only are they naturally friendly and even-tempered, but they actually like to spend time with people. If raised from a kid, these goats can form close bonds with their human caretakers. Nigerian Dwarf Goats also have the benefit of being smaller than many goat breeds so they take up less space and require less food.

Q: What do I need besides an enclosure for my goats?

Chapter Ten: Frequently Asked Questions

A: In addition to the fenced enclosure itself, you will also
need to provide your goats with shelter. To feed your goats,
you will need a hayrack – hayracks keep the hay off the
ground and prevent your goats from soiling the hay. As far
as equipment goes, you may want to invest in a pair of hoof
trimmers – if you plan to breed goats, you may also want to
think about a disbudding iron.

Buying Nigerian Dwarf Goats

Q: What are the benefits of adopting a goat?
A: Adopting a Nigerian Dwarf Goat rather than purchasing
from a breeder can save you a lot of money. There is also
the benefit that the goat is likely to have been disbudded
and, in the case of male goats, castrated already. If you are
lucky, the goat has also been vaccinated – all of these things
will save you a lot of time and money in the long run.

Q: What should I do before buying a goat?
A: Before you go out and buy a Nigerian Dwarf Goat, you
need to be absolutely sure you can handle the commitment.
Caring for goats is an everyday job – you need to provide
your goats with food and fresh water, not to mention
veterinary care and proper shelter. It takes time and effort
to maintain your goat enclosure and you cannot leave your
goats alone for extended periods of time.

If you have decided that a Nigerian Dwarf Goat is the right pet for you, there are still a few things you need to do before buying one. You must set up the enclosure and stock up on food so you are prepared for your goats when you bring them home. If you live in the U.K. you will need to obtain the proper permits and fill out the Animal Moving License with your chosen breeder.

Housing Nigerian Dwarf Goats

Q: Can I keep Nigerian Dwarf Goats in a dog house?
A: You can use a large dog house as a shelter for your Nigerian Dwarf Goats, but you cannot keep them there exclusively. These goats require plenty of space to run and play – they will not thrive if they are confined indoors for extended periods of time. If you are only using the dog house as shelter from rain and cold weather, however, it is completely acceptable as long as the dog house is large enough to accommodate all of your goats comfortably.

Q: Why can't I let my goats roam free?
A: If you live on a large plot of land, you may be tempted to simply let your goats wander. There are two dangers associated with doing this. First, your goats may wander too far and become lost – they may even wander into the

road and be hit by a car. Second, your goats will be vulnerable to predators if they are not kept in a secure enclosure.

Q: Can I keep Nigerian Dwarf Goats in a backyard homestead?

A: Raising backyard goats is quickly becoming an urban trend. Nigerian Dwarf Goats are a suitable and popular choice for many – under the right conditions. These dairy goats not only make great pets, but – as stated earlier – allow people who want to be in charge of their food sources to produce nutritious goat's milk, goat's milk cheese, as well as homemade goat's milk soap. Because of their diminutive size, they are a good pet for a smaller yard, as long as you are aware that they cannot be left alone for a significant period of time and they need to be milked twice daily. Also, keep in mind that female dairy goats need to get pregnant and give birth in order to produce milk so this means dealing with male companions and caring for their kids when they are born. A lot of responsibilities go along with this, so it's best to consult a homestead community in your area with experience raising them for guidance on the best decision for you. Overall, they are wonderful city pets, provided they are legal and far enough away from neighbors. A good fence to ensure they stay within boundaries, as well as one that is constructed for their safety, is essential.

Feeding Nigerian Dwarf Goats

Q: Will my goats be okay if I only feed them commercial pellets?

A: No. Fresh hay is an essential part of your goat's diet and they will not thrive without it. Ideally, fresh hay should compose 50% of your goats' diet and commercial pellets should only be used as a supplement.

Q: Can I let my goats graze in the yard or pasture?

A: Goats are natural foragers so, if given the opportunity, they will be eager to do so. You should be careful, however, before you let your goats graze. There are certain plants which are toxic to goats so you should check your yard or pasture first to be sure it is safe.

Q: How much water do Nigerian Dwarf Goats need?

A: Nigerian Dwarf Goats can drink up to 6 gallons (27 liters) of water per day. It is important that you provide a constant source of fresh water for your goats. Nigerian Dwarf Goats will not drink water that has been soiled, so you may need to check the troughs several times and refill them daily.

Breeding Nigerian Dwarf Goats

Q: How often can I breed my Nigerian Dwarf Goats?
A: Though Nigerian Dwarf Goats can technically be bred year-round, you need to be careful not to exhaust them. A one or two year-old buck should only be mated 25 times per year while an older buck can be used to service does up to 75 times. Many experienced goat owners recommend not mating a single doe more than three times in a two-year period.

Q: Why can't I bring my buck to the doe for breeding?
A: Most breeders recommend that you bring the doe into the buck's enclosure for breeding. If you do it the other way around, the buck may be distracted or stressed by the change in environment and could be less likely to mate with the doe. Also, the buck is likely to have engaged in urine-spraying, making himself and his environment more appealing to a doe.

Chapter Eleven: Relevant Websites

1.) Food for Nigerian Dwarf Goats

United States Websites:

"Nutrition of Goats." The Merck Veterinary Manual.
<http://www.merckmanuals.com/vet>

Ace, Donald L. "Feeding and Housing Dairy Goats."
University of Missouri Extension.
<http://extension.missouri.edu/publications/DisplayPub.asp
x?P=G3990>

"Feeding Goats." University of Connecticut Extension.
<http://www.extension.uconn.edu/pages/department/litchfield/documents/FeedingGoats.pdf>

United Kingdom Websites:

"Supplementation of On-Farm Goats." Department for International Development.
<http://r4d.dfid.gov.uk/PDF/Outputs/R7351h.pdf>

"Feeding Goats for First-Timers." FancyFeed Company Ltd.
<http://www.fancyfeedcompany.co.uk/library:14.htm>

"Natural Food for Goats." Pet Samaritans.
<http://www.petsamaritans.co.uk/feeding-goats/>

"Goat Feeding." WoodGreen.
<http://www.woodgreen.org.uk/pet_advice/489_goat_feeding>

2.) Care for Nigerian Dwarf Goats

United States Websites:

Johnson, Sherry. "Goat Care." Grasse Acres Nigerian Dwarf Goats. <http://grasseacres.com/care>

"Nigerian Dwarf Goat." The American Livestock Breeds Conservancy. <http://www.albc-usa.org/cpl/nigerian.html>

"Nigerian Dwarf Goats." Goats 4H. <http://www.goats4h.com/Dwarf.html>

"Nigerian Dwarf Dairy Goats." Dairy Goat Journal. <http://www.dairygoatjournal.com/goats/nigeriandwarf/>

United Kingdom Websites:

"Goats as Pets." Goat Care and Goat Products. <http://www.goats.co.uk/Goats_as_Pets.htm>

"A Guide to Looking After Goats." Pet Samaritans. <http://www.petsamaritans.co.uk/goat-keeping-a-beginners-guide/>

"How to Choose and Keep Goats." CountryWide. <http://www.countrywidefarmers.co.uk/pws/Content.ice?page=GuidesChooseKeepGoats&pgForward=businesscontentfull>

"An Introduction to Your Goat." Longdown Farm. <http://www.longdownfarm.co.uk/uploads/pdf/care>

3.) Health Info for Nigerian Dwarf Goats

United States Websites:

"Overview of Health-Management Interaction: Goats." The Merck Veterinary Manual. <http://www.merckmanuals.com/vet>

"Common Diseases of Goats." The Merck Veterinary Manual. <http://www.merckmanuals.com/vet>

Pezzanite, Lynn. "Common Diseases and Health Problems in Sheep and Goats." Purdue University Extension. <http://www.extension.purdue.edu/extmedia/AS/AS-595-commonDiseases.pdf>

Jones, Steve. "Herd Health Program for Dairy Goats." University of Arkansas Division of Agriculture. <http://www.uaex.edu/other_areas/publications/pdf/fsa-4006.pdf>

United Kingdom Websites:

"Sheep and Goats: Health Regulations." Department for Environment, Food and Rural Affairs.

<https://www.gov.uk/monitoring-prevention-and-control-of-disease>

"Goat Health." British Goat Society. <http://www.allgoats.org.uk/Goathealth.htm>

"An Introduction to Goat Keeping." Animal Welfare Foundation. <http://www.bva-awf.org.uk/sites/bva-awf.org.uk/files/user/introduction_to_goat_keeping.pdf>

4.) General Info for Nigerian Dwarf Goats

United States Websites:

"Nigerian Dwarf Dairy Goats." Dairy Goat Journal.
<http://www.dairygoatjournal.com/goats/nigeriandwarf/>

"About Nigerian Dairy Goats." Nigerian Dwarf Goat
Association. <http://www.ndga.org/about.html>

"Breed History of the Nigerian Dwarf Dairy Goat."
American Nigerian Dwarf Dairy Association.
<http://www.andda.org/nigerians.html>

United Kingdom Websites:

Davis, Brenna. "Differences Between Pygmy, Miniature and
Dwarf Goats." eHow UK.
<http://www.ehow.co.uk/info_8732052_differences-pygmy-
miniature>

"Breed Standard." Nigerian Dwarf Goat Association.
<http://www.ndga.org/breedstandard.html>

"Keeping a Goat as a Pet." InBrief. <http://www.inbrief.co.uk/animal-law/pet-goats.htm>

5.) BreedingNigerian Dwarf Goats

United States Websites:

"Breeding and Kidding Management in the Goat Herd." NCSU Department of Animal Science. <http://www.cals.ncsu.edu/an_sci/extension/animal/meatgo at/MGBrdKidd.htm>

Gary, Lockie. "Successfully Breeding Goats." University of Florida IFAS Extension. <http://smallfarms.ifas.ufl.edu/alternative_enterprises/Artic les/Article05-Gary.pdf>

Applegate, Leslie A. "A Beginner's Guide to Breeding Your Goat." The Goat Source. <http://www.goatsource.com/Breeding%20Your%20Goat.p df>

"Dairy Goat Breeding." American Dairy Goat Association. <http://www.adga.org/index.php?option=com_content&vie w=article&id=183:dairy-goat-breeding>

United Kingdom Websites:

"Goat Breeding." Goats.co.uk.
<http://www.goats.co.uk/Goat_Breeding.htm>

"Breeding." Goats Care Guide published by the Royal Society for the Prevention of Cruelty to Animals.
<http://www.rspca.org.uk/ImageLocator/LocateAsset?asset=document&assetId=1232713000349&mode=prd>

"Goat Reproduction." Animal Corner.
<http://www.animalcorner.co.uk/farm/goats/goat_reproduction.html>

Index

Photo Credits

Cover Page, By Flickr user Jean,
<http://www.flickr.com/photos/7326810@N08/1806585487/>

Page 1, By Ltshears (Own work) [CC-BY-SA-3.0
(http://creativecommons.org/licenses/by-sa/3.0) or GFDL
(http://www.gnu.org/copyleft/fdl.html)], via Wikimedia
Commons<http://commons.wikimedia.org/wiki/
File:Nigerian_Dwarf_Goat_0651.jpg>

Page 2, By Dlanglois, via Wikimedia Commons
<http://commons.wikimedia.org/wiki/File:Nigerian_Dwarf_
Goat_01.jpg>

Page 5, By Flickr user Greg Goebel,
<http://www.flickr.com/photos/37467370@N08/7621338782/

Page 8, By USAID [Public domain], via Wikimedia
Commons, <http://commons.wikimedia.org/wiki/
File:Kabala_goats.jpg>

Page 10, By Flickr user Cliff,
<http://www.flickr.com/photos/nostri-imago/3016924674/>

Page 13, By Steven Walling (Own work) [CC-BY-SA-3.0
(http://creativecommons.org/licenses/by-sa/3.0)], via
Wikimedia Commons

<https://commons.wikimedia.org/wiki/File:Nigerian_Dwarf
_goat,_SF_zoo.jpg>

Page 15, By Flickr user Heather Paul,
<http://www.flickr.com/photos/warriorwoman531/61820925
31/>

Page 17, By Ltshears - Trisha M Shears (Own work) [Public
domain], via Wikimedia Commons,
<http://commons.wikimedia.org/wiki/File:African_Pygmy_
Goat_003.jpg>

Page 19, By Dlandlois, via Wikimedia Commons,
<http://commons.wikimedia.org/wiki/File:Nigerian_Dwarf_
Goat_02.jpg>

Page 24, By Adityamadhav83 (Own work) [CC-BY-SA-3.0
(http://creativecommons.org/licenses/by-sa/3.0)], via
Wikimedia Commons

Page 26, By Flickr user Joe Thomiessen,
<http://www.flickr.com/photos/thomissen/7503205070/>

Page 27, Courtesy of FreeDigitalPhotos.net

Page 37, By Ryan Somma (Lucy, Nigerian Dwarf Goat, and)
[CC-BY-SA-2.0 (http://creativecommons.org/licenses/by-
sa/2.0)], via Wikimedia Commons, <http://commons.
wikimedia.org/wiki/File:Pair_of_goats.jpg>

Page 57, By Flickr user Miki James, <http://www.flickr.com/photos/mikijames/26006642/sizes/o/in/photostream/>

Page 60, By DeviantArt user Sckocki, <http://sckoki.deviantart.com/art/A-little-goat-146511078>

Page 63, By Flickr user Cliff, <http://www.flickr.com/photos/nostri-imago/3016917816/>

Page 73, By U.S. Navy photo by Mass Communication Specialist 2nd Class Roger S. Duncan [Public domain], via Wikimedia Commons

Page 75, By Pixabay user Hans, <http://pixabay.com/en/goat-young-animal-horns>

Page 77, By U.S. Navy photo by Journalist Seaman Ryan Clement [Public domain], via Wikimedia Commons, <http://commons.wikimedia.org/wiki/File:US_Navy_060616 -N-3153C-047_Army_Spc._Becky_Holmbeck,_ a_veterinarian>

Page 82, By Pixabay user Hans, <http://pixabay.com/en/ domestic-goat-goat-livestock-farm-7455/>

Page 85, By Flickr user Cliff, <http://www.flickr.com/photos/nostri-imago/3016085103/>

Page 88, By Jmkarohl (Own work) [GFDL (http://www.gnu.org/copyleft/fdl.html) or CC-BY-SA-3.0-2.5-2.0-1.0 (http://creativecommons.org/licenses/by-sa/3.0)],

via Wikimedia Commons,
<http://commons.wikimedia.org/wiki/File:NigerianDwarfD airyGoat.jpg>

Page 90, By Cro-cop2, via Wikimedia Commons,
<http://commons.wikimedia.org/wiki/File:Geiten_-_Koze_- _Goats.JPG>

Page 91, By Pixabay user Beeki, <http://pixabay.com/en/ goat-goats-animal-mammals-farm-44322/>

Page 92, By Pixabay user Beeki, <http://pixabay.com/en/ goat-goats-animal-mammals-farm-44324/>

Page 94, By Flickr user Its4WildCat,
<http://www.flickr.com/photos/82193226@N00/6049529531/

Page 99, By Korall (Own work) [CC-BY-SA-3.0
(http://creativecommons.org/licenses/by-sa/3.0) or GFDL
(http://www.gnu.org/copyleft/fdl.html)], via Wikimedia
Commons, <http://commons.wikimedia.org/
wiki/File:African_dwarf_goat_baby.JPG>

References

"2012 ADGA Guidebook." American Dairy Goat Association. <http://www.adga.org/pages_adga/guidebook/GB_2012.pdf>

"About Goats." Dairy Goat Journal. <http://www.dairygoatjournal.com/about_goats/>

"About Nigerian Dairy Goats." Nigerian Dwarf Goat Association. <http://www.ndga.org/about.html>

"An Introduction to Goat Keeping." Animal Welfare Foundation. <http://www.bva-awf.org.uk/sites/bva-awf.org.uk/files/user/introduction_to_goat_keeping.pdf>

"Breed History of the Nigerian Dwarf Dairy Goat." American Nigerian Dwarf Dairy Association. <http://www.andda.org/nigerians.html>

"Breeder Directory." American Nigerian Dwarf Dairy Association. <http://www.andda.org/breeders>

"Common Diseases of Goats." The Merck Veterinary Manual. <http://www.merckmanuals.com/vet>

"Current Legal Requirements." Pygmy Goat Club. <http://www.pygmygoatclub.org/general_info/legal_reqs.htm>

"Goats: Introduction to Welfare and Ownership." The Royal Society for the Prevention of Cruelty to Animals." <http://www.rspca.org.uk/ImageLocator/LocateAsset?asset =document&assetId=1232713000349&mode=prd>

Grant, Jenny. "How to Legalize Goats in Your City." Grist. <http://grist.org/food>

"How Much Does a Pet Goat Cost?" CostHelper. <http://pets>

"How to Trim Goat Hooves the Right Way." Boer Goats. <http://www.boergoatshome.com/hooves>

Johnson, Sherry. "Goat Care." Grasse Acres Nigerian Dwarf Goats. <http://grasseacres.com/care>

Jones, Steve. "Herd Health Program for Dairy Goats." University of Arkansas Division of Agriculture. <http://www.uaex.edu/other_areas/publications/pdf/fsa-4006.pdf>

"Male Goat Information: Bucks & Wethers." Fias Co Farm. <http://fiascofarm.com/goats/buck>

Mendell, Mac. "Housing for Dairy Goats." Purdue University Department of Animal Sciences. <http://www.ansc.purdue.edu/goat/factsheet/housing>

"Nigerian Dwarf Goat." The American Livestock Breeds Conservancy. <http://www.albc-usa.org/cpl/nigerian.html>

"Nigerian Dwarf Goats." Goats 4H. <http://www.goats4h.com/Dwarf.html>

"Nigerian Dwarf Dairy Goats." Dairy Goat Journal. <http://www.dairygoatjournal.com/goats/nigeriandwarf/>

"Nutrition of Goats." The Merck Veterinary Manual. <http://www.merckmanuals.com/vet>

"Overview of Health-Management Interaction: Goats." The Merck Veterinary Manual. <http://www.merckmanuals.com/vet>

Pezzanite, Lynn. "Common Diseases and Health Problems in Sheep and Goats." Purdue University Extension. <http://www.extension.purdue.edu/extmedia/AS/AS-595-commonDiseases.pdf>

"Polled and Horned Genetics." Nigerian Dwarf Colors. <http://nigeriandwarfcolors.weebly.com/polledhorned-genetics.html>

"Private Goat Ownership." Public Health – Seattle and King County. <http://www.kingcounty.gov/healthservices/health>

"Sheep and Goats: Health Regulations." Department for Environment, Food and Rural Affairs.

<https://www.gov.uk/monitoring-prevention-and-control-of-disease>

"The Nigerian Dwarf in America." American Nigerian Dwarf Dairy Association. <http://www.andda.org/forms/ANDDAbrochure.pdf>

"Urban Goats." Chicago Farm and Table. <http://www.chicagofarmandtable.com/2012/05/31/goats-in-chicago/>

Made in the USA
Lexington, KY
04 November 2014